McBroom's Wonderful One-Acre Farm

ILLUSTRATED BY QUENTIN BLAKE

SID FLEISCHMAN

McBroom's Wonderful One-Acre Farm

THREE TALL TALES

GREENWILLOW BOOKS
NEW YORK

Library of Congress Cataloging-in-Publication Data

Fleischman, Sid (date)
McBroom's wonderful one-acre farm / by Sid Fleischman
pictures by Quentin Blake.
p.   cm.
Summary: Three humorous adventures on McBroom's
wonderful one-acre prairie farm.
ISBN 0-688-11159-9
[1. Farms—Fiction.   2. Humorous stories.
3. Tall tales.]   I. Blake, Quentin, Ill.
PZ7.F5992Mah   1992
[Fic]—dc20   91-31906   CIP   AC

CONTENTS

McBROOM TELLS THE TRUTH

There has been so much tomfool nonsense told about McBroom's wonderful one-acre farm that I had better set matters straight. I'm McBroom. Josh McBroom. I'll explain about the watermelons in a minute.

I aim to put down the facts, one after the other, the way things happened—exactly.

It began, you might say, the day we left the farm in Connecticut. We piled our youngsters and everything we owned in our old air-cooled Franklin automobile. We headed west.

To count noses, in addition to my own, there was my dear wife, Melissa, and our eleven redheaded, freckle-faced youngsters. Their names were Will*jill*hester*chester*peter*polly*tim*tom*mary*larry*andlittle*clarinda*.

It was summer, and the trees along the way were full of birdsong. We had got as far as Iowa when my dear wife, Melissa, made a startling discovery. We had *twelve* children along—one too many! She had just counted them again.

I slammed on the brakes and raised a cloud of dust.

"Will*jill*hester*chester* peter*polly* tim*tom* mary*larry* andlit-tle*clarinda*!" I shouted. "Line up!"

The youngsters tumbled out of the car. I counted noses, and there were twelve. I counted again. Twelve. It was a baffler as all the faces were familiar. Once more I made the count—but this time I caught Larry slipping around behind. He was having his nose counted twice, and the mystery was solved. The scamp! Didn't we laugh, though, and stretch our legs in the bargain.

Just then a thin, long-legged man came ambling down the road. He was so scrawny I do believe he

could have hidden behind a flagpole, ears and all. He wore a tall, stiff collar, a diamond stickpin in his tie, and a black hat.

"Lost, neighbor?" he asked, spitting out the pips of a green apple he was eating.

"Not a bit," said I. "We're heading west, sir. We gave up our farm—it was half rocks and the other half tree stumps. Folks tell us there's land out west and the sun shines in the winter."

The stranger pursed his lips. "You can't beat Iowa for farmland," he said.

"Maybe so." I nodded. "But I'm short of funds. Unless they're giving farms away in Iowa, we'll keep a-going."

The man scratched his chin. "See here, I've got more land than I can plow. You look like nice folks. I'd like to have you for neighbors. I'll let you have eighty acres cheap. Not a stone or a tree stump anywhere on the place. Make me an offer."

"Thank you kindly, sir." I smiled. "But I'm afraid you would laugh at me if I offered you everything in my leather purse."

"How much is that?"

"Ten dollars exactly."

"Sold!" he said.

Well, I almost choked with surprise. I thought he must be joking, but quick as a flea he was scratching out a deed on the back of an old envelope.

"Hector Jones is my name, neighbor," he said. "You can call me Heck—everyone does."

Was there ever a more kindly and generous man? He signed the deed with a flourish, and I gladly opened the clasp of my purse.

Three milky white moths flew out. They had been gnawing on the ten-dollar bill all the way from Connecticut, but enough remained to buy the farm. And not a stone or tree stump on it!

Mr. Heck Jones jumped on the running board and guided us a mile up the road. My youngsters tried to amuse him along the way. Will wiggled his ears, and Jill crossed her eyes, and Chester twitched his nose like a rabbit, but I reckoned Mr. Jones wasn't used to youngsters. Hester flapped her arms like a bird, Peter whistled through his front teeth, which were missing, and Tom tried to stand on his head in the back of the car. Mr. Heck Jones ignored them all.

Finally he raised his long arm and pointed.

"There's your property, neighbor," he said.

Didn't we tumble out of the car in a hurry? We gazed with delight at our new farm. It was broad and sunny, with an oak tree on a gentle hill. There was one defect, to be sure. A boggy-looking pond spread across an acre beside the road. You could lose a cow in a place like that, but we had got a bargain—no doubt about it.

"Mama," I said to my dear Melissa. "See that fine old oak on the hill? That's where we'll build our farmhouse."

"No, you won't," said Mr. Heck Jones. "That oak ain't on your property."

"But, sir—"

"All that's yours is what you see underwater. Not a rock or a tree stump in it, like I said."

I thought he must be having his little joke, except that there wasn't a smile to be found on his face. "But, *sir!*" I said. "You clearly stated that the farm was eighty acres."

"That's right."

"That marshy pond hardly covers an acre."

"That's wrong," he said. "There are a full eighty acres—one piled on the other, like griddle cakes. I didn't say your farm was all on the surface. It's eighty acres deep, McBroom. Read the deed."

I read the deed. It was true.

"Hee-haw! Hee-haw!" he snorted. "I got the best of you, McBroom! Good day, neighbor."

He scurried away, laughing up his sleeve all the way home. I soon learned that Mr. Heck was always laughing up his sleeve. Folks told me that when he'd hang up his coat and go to bed, all that stored-up laughter would pour out his sleeve and keep him awake nights. But there's no truth to that.

I'll tell you about the watermelons in a minute.

Well, there we stood gazing at our one-acre farm that wasn't good for anything but jumping into on a hot day. And the day was the hottest I could remember. The hottest on record, as it turned out. That was the day, three minutes before noon, when the cornfields all over Iowa exploded into popcorn. That's history. You must have read about that. There are pictures to prove it.

I turned to my children. "Will*jill*hester*chester*peter-

13

*polly*tim*tom*mary*larry*andlittle*clarinda,*" I said. "There's always a bright side to things. That pond we bought is a mite muddy, but it's wet. Let's jump in and cool off."

That idea met with favor, and we were soon in our swimming togs. I gave the signal, and we took a running jump. At that moment such a dry spell struck that we landed in an acre of dry earth. The pond had evaporated. It was very surprising.

My boys had jumped in headfirst, and there was

nothing to be seen of them but their legs kicking in the air. I had to pluck them out of the earth like carrots. Some of my girls were still holding their noses. Of course, they were sorely disappointed to have that swimming hole pulled out from under them.

But the moment I ran the topsoil through my fingers, my farmer's heart skipped a beat. That pond bottom felt as soft and rich as black silk. "My dear Melissa!" I called. "Come look! This topsoil is so rich it ought to be kept in a bank."

I was in a sudden fever of excitement. That glorious topsoil seemed to cry out for seed. My dear Melissa had a sack of dried beans along, and I sent Will and Chester to fetch it. I saw no need to bother plowing the field. I directed Polly to draw a straight furrow with a stick and Tim to follow her, poking holes in the ground. Then I came along. I dropped a bean in each hole and stamped on it with my heel.

Well, I had hardly gone a couple of yards when something green and leafy tangled my foot. I looked behind me. There was a beanstalk traveling along in a hurry and looking for a pole to climb on.

"Glory be!" I exclaimed. That soil was *rich*! The

But we found out that corn was positively dangerous to plant. The stalk shot up so fast it would skin your nose.

Of course, there was a secret to that topsoil. A government man came out and made a study of the matter. He said there had once been a huge lake in that part of Iowa. It had taken thousands of years to shrink up to our pond, as you can imagine. The lake fish must have got packed in worse than sardines. There's nothing like fish to put nitrogen in the soil. That's a scientific fact. Nitrogen makes things grow to beat all. And we did occasionally turn up a fish bone.

It wasn't long before Mr. Heck Jones came around to pay us a neighborly call. He was eating a raw turnip. When he saw the way we were planting and harvesting cabbage, his eyes popped out of his head. It almost cost him his eyesight.

He scurried away, muttering to himself.

"My dear Melissa," I said. "That man is up to mischief."

Folks in town had told me that Mr. Heck Jones had the worst farmland in Iowa. He couldn't give it away.

Tornado winds had carried off his topsoil and left the hardpan right on top. He had to plow it with wedges and a sledgehammer. One day we heard a lot of booming on the other side of the hill, and my youngsters went up to see what was happening. It turned out he was planting seeds with a shotgun.

Meanwhile, we went about our business on the farm. I don't mind saying that before long we were showing a handsome profit. Back in Connecticut we had been lucky to harvest one crop a year. Now we were planting and harvesting three, four crops a *day*.

But there were things we had to be careful about. Weeds, for one thing. My youngsters took turns standing weed guard. The instant a weed popped out of the ground, they'd race to it and hoe it to death. You can imagine what would happen if weeds ever got going in rich soil like ours.

We also had to be careful about planting time. Once we planted lettuce just before my dear Melissa rang the noon bell for dinner. While we ate, the lettuce headed up and went to seed. We lost the whole crop.

One day back came Mr. Heck Jones with a grin on

his face. He had figured out a loophole in the deed that made the farm ours.

"*Hee-haw!*" he laughed. He was munching a radish. "I got the best of you now, Neighbor McBroom. The deed says you were to pay me *everything* in your purse, and you *didn't*."

"On the contrary, sir," I answered. "Ten dollars. There wasn't another cent in my purse."

"There were *moths* in the purse. I seen 'em flutter out. Three milky white moths, McBroom. I want three moths by three o'clock this afternoon, or I aim to take back the farm. *Hee-haw!*"

And off he went, laughing up his sleeve.

Mama was just ringing the noon bell so we didn't have much time. Confound that man! But he did have his legal point.

"Will*jill*hester*chester*peter*polly*tim*tom*mary*larry*andlittle*clarinda!*" I said. "We've got to catch three milky white moths! Hurry!"

We hurried in all directions. But moths are next to impossible to locate in the daytime. Try it yourself. Each of us came back empty-handed.

My dear Melissa began to cry, for we were sure to

lose our farm. I don't mind telling you that things looked dark. Dark! That was it! I sent the youngsters running down the road to a lonely old pine tree and told them to rush back with a bushel of pinecones.

Didn't we get busy, though! We planted a pinecone every three feet. They began to grow. We stood around anxiously, and I kept looking at my pocket watch. I'll tell you about the watermelons in a moment.

Sure enough, by ten minutes to three, those cones had grown into a thick pine forest.

It was dark inside, too! Not a ray of sunlight slipped through the green pine boughs. Deep in the forest I lit a lantern. Hardly a minute passed before I was surrounded by milky white moths—they thought it was night. I caught three on the wing and rushed out of the forest.

There stood Mr. Heck Jones waiting with the sheriff to foreclose.

"Hee-haw! Hee-haw!" old Heck laughed. He was eating a quince apple. "It's nigh onto three o'clock, and you can't catch moths in the daytime. The farm is mine!"

"Not so fast, Neighbor Jones," said I, with my hands

cupped together. "Here are the three moths. Now ske-daddle, sir, before your feet take root and poison ivy grows out of your ears!"

He scurried away, muttering to himself.

"My dear Melissa," I said. "That man is up to mis-chief. He'll be back."

It took a good bit of work to clear the timber, I'll tell you. We had some of the pine milled and built our-selves a house on the corner of the farm. What was left we gave away to our neighbors. We were weeks blasting the roots out of the ground.

But I don't want you to think there was nothing but work on our farm. Some crops we grew just for the fun of it. Take pumpkins. The vines grew so fast we could hardly catch the pumpkins. It was something to see. The youngsters used to wear themselves out running after those pumpkins. Sometimes they'd have pumpkin races.

Sunday afternoons, just for the sport of it, the older boys would plant a pumpkin seed and try to catch a ride. It wasn't easy. You had to grab hold the instant the blossom dropped off and the pumpkin began to

swell. Whoosh! It would yank you off your feet and take you whizzing over the farm until it wore itself out. Sometimes they'd use banana squash, which was faster.

And the girls learned to ride cornstalks like pogo sticks. It was just a matter of standing over the kernel as the stalk came busting up through the ground. It was good for quite a bounce.

We'd see Mr. Heck Jones standing on the hill in the distance, watching. He wasn't going to rest until he had pried us off our land.

Then, late one night, I was awakened by a hee-hawing outside the house. I went to the window and saw old Heck in the moonlight. He was cackling and chuckling and heeing and hawing and sprinkling seed every which way.

I pulled off my sleeping cap and rushed outside.

"What mischief are you up to, Neighbor Jones!" I shouted.

"Hee-haw!" he answered, and scurried away, laughing up his sleeve.

I had a sleepless night, as you can imagine. The next morning, as soon as the sun came up, that farm of ours broke out in weeds. You never saw such weeds! They heaved out of the ground and tumbled madly

over each other—chickweed and milkweed, thistles and wild morning glory. In no time at all the weeds were in a tangle several feet thick and still rising.

We had a fight on our hands, I tell you! "Will*jill*hester*chester*peter*polly*tim*tom*mary*larry*andlittle*clarinda*!" I shouted. "There's work to do!"

We started hoeing and hacking away. For every weed we uprooted, another reseeded itself. We were a solid month battling those weeds. If our neighbors hadn't pitched in to help, we'd still be there burning weeds.

The day finally came when the farm was cleared and up popped old Heck Jones. He was eating a big slice of watermelon. That's what I was going to tell you about.

"Howdy, Neighbor McBroom," he said. "I came to say good-bye."

"Are you leaving, sir?" I asked.

"No, but *you* are."

I looked him squarely in the eye. "And if I don't, sir?"

"Why, *hee-haw*, McBroom! There's heaps more of weed seed where that came from!"

My dander was up. I rolled back my sleeves, meaning to give him a whipping he wouldn't forget. But what happened next saved me the bother.

As my youngsters gathered around, Mr. Heck Jones made the mistake of spitting out a mouthful of watermelon seeds.

Things did happen fast!

Before I had quite realized what he had done, a watermelon vine whipped up around old Heck's scrawny legs and jerked him off his feet. He went whizzing every which way over the farm. Watermelon seeds were flying. Soon he came zipping back and collided with a pumpkin left over from Sunday. In no time watermelons and pumpkins went galloping all over the place, and they were knocking him about something wild. He streaked here and there. Melons crashed and exploded. Old Heck was so covered with melon pulp he looked like he had been shot out of a ketchup bottle.

It was something to see. Will stood there wiggling his ears. Jill crossed her eyes. Chester twitched his nose. Hester flapped her arms like a bird. Peter whistled through his front teeth, which had grown in. Tom stood on his head. And little Clarinda took her first step.

By then the watermelons and pumpkins began to play themselves out. I figured Mr. Heck Jones would like to get home as fast as possible. So I asked Larry to fetch me the seed of a large banana squash.

"*Hee-haw!* Neighbor Jones," I said, and pitched the seed at his feet. I hardly had time to say good-bye before the vine had him. A long banana squash gave him a fast ride all the way home. I wish you could have been there to see it.

That's the entire truth of the matter. Anything else you hear about McBroom's wonderful one-acre farm is an outright fib.

MCBROOM AND THE BIG WIND

I can't deny it—it does get a mite windy out here on the prairie. Why, just last year a blow came ripping across our farm and carried off a pail of sweet milk. The next day it came back for the cow.

But that wasn't the howlin', scowlin', almighty big wind I aim to tell you about. That was just a common little prairie breeze. No-account, really. Hardly worth bragging about.

It was the *big* wind that broke my leg. I don't expect you to believe that—yet. I'd best start with some smaller weather and work up to that bonebreaker.

I remember distinctly the first prairie wind that came scampering along after we bought our wonderful one-acre farm. My, that land is rich. Best topsoil in the country. There isn't a thing that won't grow in our rich topsoil, and fast as lightning.

The morning I'm talking about, our oldest boys were helping me to shingle the roof. I had bought a keg of nails, but it turned out those nails were a whit short. We buried them in our wonderful topsoil and watered them down. In five or ten minutes those nails grew a full half inch.

So there we were, up on the roof, hammering down shingles. There wasn't a cloud in the sky at first. The younger boys were shooting marbles all over the farm, and the girls were jumping rope.

When I had pounded down the last shingle, I said to myself, "Josh McBroom, that's a mighty stout roof. It'll last a hundred years."

Just then I felt a small draft on the back of my neck. A moment later one of the girls—it was Polly, as I recall—shouted up to me. "Pa," she said, "do jackrabbits have wings?"

I laughed. "No, Polly."

"Then how come there's a flock of jackrabbits flying over the house?"

I looked up. Mercy! Rabbits were flapping their ears across the sky in a perfect V formation, northbound. I knew then we were in for a slight blow.

"Run, everybody!" I shouted to the young'uns. I didn't want the wind picking them up by the ears. "Will*jill*hester*chester*peter*polly*tim*tom*mary*larry*and-little*clarinda*—in the house! Scamper!"

The clothesline was already beginning to whip around like a jump rope. My dear wife, Melissa, who had been baking a heap of biscuits, threw open the door. In we dashed, and not a moment too soon. The wind was snapping at our heels like a pack of wolves. It aimed to barge right in and make itself at home! A prairie wind has no manners at all.

We slammed the door in its teeth. Now the wind didn't take that politely. It rammed and battered at the

work for us. I made a wind plow. I rigged a bed sheet and tackle to our old farm plow. Soon as a breeze sprang up I'd go tacking to and fro over the farm, plowing as I went. Our son Chester once plowed the entire farm in under three minutes.

On Thanksgiving morning Mama told the girls to pluck a large turkey for dinner. They didn't much like that chore, but a prairie gust arrived just in time. The girls stuck the turkey out the window. The wind plucked that turkey clean, pinfeathers and all.

Oh, we got downright glad to see a blow come along. The young'uns were always wanting to go out and play in the wind, but Mama was afraid they'd be carried off. So I made them wind shoes—made 'em out of heavy iron skillets. Out in the breeze those shoes felt light as feathers. The girls would jump rope with the clothesline. The wind spun the rope, of course.

Many a time I saw the youngsters put on their wind shoes and go clumping outside with a big tin funnel and all the empty bottles and jugs they could round up. They'd cork the containers jam full of prairie wind.

Then, come summer, when there wasn't a breath of air, they'd uncork a bottle or two of fresh winter wind and enjoy the cool breeze.

Of course, we had to windproof the farm every fall. We'd plant the field in buttercups. My, they were slippery—all that butter, I guess. The wind would slip and slide over the farm without being able to get a purchase on the topsoil. By then the boys and I had re-shingled the roof. We used screws instead of nails.

Mercy! Then came the *big* wind!

It started out gently enough. There were a few jack-rabbits and some crows flying backward through the air. Nothing out of the ordinary.

Of course, the girls went outside to jump the clothesline and the boys got busy laying up bottles of wind for summer. Mama had just baked a batch of fresh biscuits. My, they did smell good! I ate a dozen or so hot out of the oven. And that turned out to be a terrible mistake.

Outside, the wind was picking up ground speed and scattering fence posts as it went.

"Will *jill* hester *chester* peter *polly* tim *tom* mary *larry* and lit- tle *clarinda*!" I shouted. "Inside, my lambs! That wind is getting ornery!"

The young'uns came trooping in and pulled off their wind shoes. And not a moment too soon. The clothesline began to whip around so fast it seemed to disappear. Then we saw a henhouse come flying through the air, with the hens still in it.

The sky was turning dark and mean. The wind came out of the far north, howling and shrieking and shaking the house. In the cupboard cups chattered in their saucers.

Soon we noticed big balls of fur rolling along the prairie like tumbleweeds. Turned out they were timber wolves from up north. And then an old hollow log came spinning across the farm and split against my chopping stump. Out rolled a black bear, and was he in a temper! He had been trying to hibernate and didn't take kindly to being awakened. He gave out a roar and looked around for somebody to chase. He saw us at the windows and decided we would do.

The mere sight of him scared the young'uns, and they huddled together, holding hands, near the fire-place.

I got down my shotgun and opened a window. That was a *mistake*! Two things happened at once. The bear was coming on, and in my haste I forgot to calculate the direction of the wind. It came shrieking along the side of the house, and when I poked the gun barrel out the window, well, the wind bent it like an angle iron. That buckshot flew due south. I found out later it brought down a brace of ducks over Mexico.

But worse than that, when I threw open the window, such a draft came in that our young'uns *were sucked up through the chimney*! Holding hands, they were carried away like a string of sausages.

Mama near fainted away. "My dear Melissa!" I exclaimed. "Don't you worry! I'll get our young'uns back!"

I fetched a rope and rushed outside. I could see the young'uns up in the sky and blowing south.

I could also see the bear, and he could see me. He gave a growl with a mouthful of teeth like rusty nails. He rose up on his hind legs and came toward me with his eyes glowing red as fire.

I didn't fancy tangling with that monster. I dodged around behind the clothesline. I kept one eye on the bear and the other on the young'uns. They were now flying over the county seat and looked hardly bigger than mayflies.

The bear charged toward me. The wind was spinning the clothesline so fast he couldn't see it. And he charged smack into it. My, didn't he begin to jump! He jumped red-hot pepper, only faster. He had got himself trapped inside the rope and couldn't jump out.

Of course, I didn't lose a moment. I began flapping my arms like a bird. That was such an enormous *big* wind I figured I could fly after the young'uns. The wind tugged and pulled at me, but it couldn't lift me an inch off the ground.

Tarnation! I had eaten too many biscuits. They were heavy as lead and weighed me down.

The young'uns were almost out of sight. I rushed to the barn for the wind plow. Once out in the breeze, the bed sheet filled with wind. Off I shot like a cannonball, plowing a deep furrow as I went.

Didn't I streak along, though! I was making better time than the young'uns. I kept my hands on the plow handles and steered around barns and farmhouses. I saw haystacks explode in the wind. If that wind got any stronger, it wouldn't surprise me to see the sun blown off course. It would set in the south at high noon.

I plowed right along and gained rapidly on the young'uns. They were still holding hands and just clearing the treetops. Before long I was within hailing distance.

"Be brave, my lambs!" I shouted. "Hold tight!"

I spurted after them until their shadows lay across my path. But the bed sheet was so swelled out with wind that I couldn't stop the plow. Before I could let go of the handles and jump off, I had sailed far *ahead* of the young'uns.

I heaved the rope into the air. "Will*jill*hester*chester*peter*polly*tim*tom*mary*larry*andlittle*clarinda*!" I shouted as they came flying overhead. "Hang on!"

Hester missed the rope, and Jill missed the rope, and so did Peter. But Will caught it. I had to dig my heels in the earth to hold them. And then I started back. The young'uns were too light for the wind. They hung in the air. I had to drag them home on the rope like balloons on a string.

Of course, it took most of the day to shoulder my way back through the wind. It was a mighty struggle, I tell you! It was near suppertime when we saw our farmhouse ahead, and that black bear was still jumping rope!

I dragged the young'uns into the house. The rascals! They had had a jolly time flying through the air and wanted to do it again! Mama put them to bed with their wind shoes on.

The wind blew all night, and the next morning that bear was still jumping rope. His tongue was hanging out, and he had lost so much weight he was skin and bones.

Finally, about midmorning, the wind got tired of

blowing one way, so it blew the other. We got to feeling sorry for that bear and cut him loose. He was so tuckered out he didn't even growl. He just pointed himself toward the tall timber to find another hollow log to crawl into. But he had lost the fine art of walking. We watched him jump, jump, jump north until he was out of sight.

That was the howlin', scowlin', all mighty *big* wind that broke my leg. It had not only pulled up fence posts, but the *holes* as well. It dropped one of those holes right outside the barn door and I stepped in it.

That's the bottom truth. Everyone on the prairie knows Josh McBroom would rather break his leg than tell a fib.

MCBROOM'S EAR

Grasshoppers—yes, they did get wind of our wonderful one-acre farm. The long-legged, saw-legged, hop-legged rascals ate us out of house and home.

You know how grasshoppers are. They'd as soon spit tobacco juice as look at you. And they're terribly hungry creatures. I guess there's nothing that can eat more in less time than a swarm of grasshoppers. Green things, especially, make their mouths water.

I don't intend to talk about it with a hee and a haw. Mercy, no! If you know me—Josh McBroom—you

know I'd as soon live in a tree as tamper with the truth.

I'd best start with the weather. Summer was just waking up, but the days weren't near warm enough yet for grasshoppers. The young'uns were helping me to dig a water well. They talked of growing one thing and another to enter in the County Fair.

I guess you've heard how amazing rich our farm is. Anything will grow in it—quick. Seeds burst in the ground, and crops shoot right up before your eyes. Why, just yesterday our oldest boy dropped a five-cent piece, and before he could find it, that nickel had grown to a quarter.

Early one morning a skinny, tangle-haired stranger came ambling along the road. My, he was tall! I do believe if his hat fell off, it would take a day or two to reach the ground.

"Howdy, sir," he said. "I'm Slim-Face John from here, there, and other places. I'll paint your barn cheap."

That man was not only tall, skinny, and tangle-haired, he was nearsighted. "We don't own a barn," I said.

He squinted and laughed. "In that case," he said, "I'll paint it free."

"Done." I smiled.

He painted that no-barn in less than a second, with time left over. He appeared to be hungry, so my dear wife, Melissa, gave him a hearty breakfast, and he went ambling away. "I'll be back." He waved.

The young'uns and I kept digging that well. My, it was hard work. They'd lower a bucket, I'd fill it with earth, and they'd haul it up like a tug-of-war. All eleven of them.

hundreds. They nibbled our cabbage and lettuce, but it was nothing to be alarmed about. We could grow vegetables faster than they could eat them—three or four crops a day.

Along about sundown the saw-legged visitors came whirring in by the hundreds and the thousands. I wasn't worried. Grasshoppers are hardly worth counting in small numbers like that.

"Pa," Chester said at breakfast. "County Fair's tomorrow. Reckon it's time to set out my watermelons."

"I'm going to grow a prize tomato," Mary declared. "Big as a balloon."

"You young'uns use the patch behind the house," I said. "I aim to plant the farm in corn."

The grasshoppers didn't get in our way. Larry and little Clarinda fed them turnip greens out of their hands. I got the field planted in no time.

My, it was fine corn-growing weather. The stalks leaped right up, dangling with ears.

Suddenly a silvery green cloud rose off the horizon and raced toward us.

Grasshoppers!

Grasshoppers by the thousands! Grasshoppers by

the millions! Little did we know it was the beginning of the Great Grasshopper War—or, as it came to be called, the War of McBroom's Ear.

"Will*jill*hester*chester*peter*polly*tim*tom*mary*larry*andlit-tle*clarinda*!" I shouted. "Brooms and branches! Shoo them off!"

We began yelling and running about and waving our weapons. The grasshoppers spun over our ripening cornfield. They feasted their eyes—and flew off.

"We—scared 'em away!" Tim declared.

"No," I said. "That was just the advance party. They went back for the main herd. *And here they come!*"

Acres of grasshoppers! Square miles of grasshoppers! They came streaking toward us like a great roaring thunderbolt of war.

"Brooms and branches!" I yelled.

The hungry devils tucked napkins under their chins and swooped down for the attack. Mercy! The air got so thick with hoppers you could swing a bucket once and fill it twice. They made a whirring, hopping, jumping fog. We could barely see a foot beyond our noses.

But we could hear the ravenous rascals. They were chomping and chewing up our cornfield and spitting out the cobs. They ate that farm right down to the ground in exactly four seconds flat.

Then they rose in the air, still hungry as wolves, and waited for the next crop.

"Pa!" Chester said. "They skinned my watermelons!"

"Pa!" Mary cried. "They didn't even wait for my prize tomatoes to ripen. They ate them green!"

"Pa!" little Clarinda said. "What happened to your socks?"

I looked down. Glory be! Those infernal dinner guests had eaten the socks right out of my shoes—green socks. All they left were the holes in the toes.

Some of the young'uns broke into tears. "We won't be able to grow anything for the County Fair!"

"We're not beat yet, my lambs," I said, thinking as hard as I could. "Those hoppers did have us outnumbered, but not outsmarted. I'm going to town for seed. Better clear away the corncobs."

I drove to town in our air-cooled Franklin automobile and was back before noon with fifty pounds of fine seed. The grasshoppers were still stretched all over the sky, waiting. The young'uns had cleared the farm, throwing the corncobs on the heap of dirt beside the well.

"Not a moment to lose," I said. "Help scatter the seed."

Before long our farm was bushed out, green as a

one-acre jungle. Those hoppers smacked their lips and fought to get at it. They whirred and swarmed and cranched and crunched—that crop disappeared as if sucked up by a tornado.

Well, you should have seen how surprised they were! That first wave of hoppers was all but breathing fire. And no wonder. They had dined on hot green peppers.

They streaked off in a hurry, looking for something to drink.

Of course, there were still tons of grasshoppers left. We kept sowing crops of hot green peppers all afternoon until there wasn't a jump-leg to be seen. We found out later they had swarmed to a lake in the next county and drunk it dry.

But they'd be back. The young'uns would have to grow their prizewinners in a hurry.

"Pa—look!" little Clarinda shouted.

She was pointing to the tall heap of dirt, littered with corncobs. Glory be! The grasshoppers had missed a lone kernel and it had taken root behind our backs. A cornstalk was growing up as big as a tree.

That dirt hill was powerful rich. The roots of that wondrous stalk were having a banquet! A single ear of corn began to form before our eyes. Big? Why, it was already fatter than a potbellied stove and still growing.

"That looks like a prizewinner to me!" I declared. "You scamps will go partners."

Jill and Hester and Polly climbed to their tree house to keep a sharp eye out for grasshoppers. That ear of corn grew longer and fatter. It was a beauty! The stalk began to bend under its weight. And it was ripening fast.

Didn't we get busy, though! We fixed loops of rope around that ear so as to let it down easy. Will climbed up a ladder with a bucksaw and went to work. It must have taken him five minutes to saw that giant ear off the stalk.

We eased it down with the ropes. I tell you, we could hardly believe our eyes. That ear of corn was so big you couldn't see it in a single glance. You had to look twice.

"Grasshoppers!" Jill shouted from the tree house. "Grasshoppers coming, Pa!"

"Quick," I said. "Into the house!"

It took all of us to lift that ear of corn. But it wouldn't fit through the door. And it wouldn't fit through the window.

"The well!" I shouted.

We lowered it by ropes and covered the well over with some rusty sheets of corrugated tin. And just in time. Those hoppers had spotted our great ear from the sky and came whirring across the farm in a green blizzard. But they couldn't get at that ear of corn.

"It's safe for the night," I said.

"How will we *ever* get it past the hoppers to the fair

tomorrow?" Mary asked.

I don't have to tell you the problem gave me a sleep-less night. About four in the morning I jumped out of bed and woke the young'uns.

"Brooms and buckets!" I said. "Follow me."

We tiptoed outside, careful not to wake the jump-legs. We quietly raised our ear of corn from the well and replaced the sheets of corrugated tin. Then I filled the buckets from the shed.

"Start painting," I whispered.

The young'uns dipped their brooms and painted that giant corn ear from end to end and all over.

At sunup the grasshoppers rose from the fields and went looking for breakfast. They headed straight for the well, banging their heads on the rusty tin. My, what a clatter! They thought our enormous big ear was still down there.

Well, it was in plain sight. Only they didn't recognize it. The husk wasn't green anymore. We had *white-washed* it.

We lifted it to the roof of the old Franklin and tied it down. "Everybody pile in." I smiled, starting up the motor. "We're off to the fair!"

Just then Mr. Slim-Face John came along.

"Howdy." He smiled. "I'll paint your farmhouse cheap."

"Oh, I'd dearly like that," Mama said. "Red, with white windowsills."

"Done," I said. "You'll find paint in the shed." And we were off.

Well, you should have seen heads turn along the way. What *was* that thing on the roof of our car? An ear of corn? No, sir! No farmer can raise corn that big. And white as chalk!

We bumped along the dirt road, following signs to the County Fair. We enjoyed the sights—barns, and silos, and cows chewing their cuds in the shade.

"How much farther?" Polly asked.

"Ten, twelve miles," I said. "Be patient."

I noticed the prairie windmills begin to turn. A hot wind was coming up, dragging a cloud with it. We could hear the rumble of thunder.

"How much farther, Pa?" Tim asked.

"Eight, ten miles," I said. "Be patient."

But I didn't like the look of that cloud. It grew darker and heavier and came blowing our way.

"Heads in!" I called to the young'uns. "Thunder-shower ahead."

We met the storm head-on. It didn't amount to much, but those raindrops were almost hot enough to scald you. They bounced like sparks off the hood. A moment later the sky was blue again and the summer shower behind us.

"How much farther, Pa?" Mary asked.

"Six, eight miles," I said. "Be patient."

"Pa," Will said. He hadn't bothered to pull his head in the window, and his hair was wet. "Pa, look what's happened to our corn!"

I jammed on the brakes and got out to see. Lo and

behold—the husk was bright green again! The summer shower had washed off the whitewash.

I jumped back behind the wheel, and off we spun. "Watch for grasshoppers," I shouted.

"I'm watching, Pa," little Clarinda answered. *"And here they come!"*

Well, it was a race. The hoppers came roaring after us in full battle formation. The old Franklin creaked and groaned and clanked, but her heart was in it. We bumped in and out of the ruts and jumped a few.

"They're gaining on us, Pa!"

I had the foot pedal to the floorboard. Soon we could see the flags and banners of the County Fair ahead.

But not soon enough. The first hop-legs were landing on the roof, and we could hear them ripping and tearing at the husk. By the time we reached the fairgrounds we'd have nothing left but the cob.

But the old Franklin started to backfire, banging and booming something fierce. Those hop-legs jumped a mile, and we made it across the fairgrounds.

I charged right into the main exhibition building

60

and jammed on the brakes. "Shut all the doors!" I shouted. "Grasshoppers! Grasshoppers coming!"

The doors swung shut, and we could breathe easy at last. Folks began to cluster around, their eyes rising as their jaws fell open at the wonder of our ear of corn. And I declare if the hungry rascals hadn't husked it neat as you please.

We lifted it down off the roof and put it on display. The judges came by and asked what name to enter it by.

"McBroom." I smiled. "Will*jill*hester*chester*peter*polly*tim*tom*mary*larry*andlittle*clarinda*—McBroom!"

Well, the judges gave it first, second, third prize and honorable mention, too. But, my, it was getting overheated in there with the doors closed.

The young'uns lined up to have their picture taken for the county paper. There was one long smile reaching from Will at one end to little Clarinda at the other. The noon sun kept beating down on the roof, and all of a sudden there came a loud bang.

I thought at first it was our tired old Franklin. But no. It was the young'uns' enormous, big prizewinning ear of corn—beginning to pop! The inside of that building had grown so infernal hot it was a perfect popcorn popper.

Well, it did get noisy in there! Kernels swelled and exploded like great white cannonballs. They bounced off the roof and the walls. Pop-pop-pop. Pop. Pop-pop-pop-pop-pop! Folks ducked, and others ran. Corn in their rows boomed away in regular broadsides! I tell you popcorn was flying all over the hall and piling up like a heavy snowfall. Pop-pop-pop-pop-pop-pop-pop-pop! In no time at all we were buried in light, fluffy popcorn. It swelled to the roof and forced open the doors. It overflowed the building at both ends.

There wasn't a grasshopper left in sight. All that ruckus had sent them flying. As far as I know, they headed for the full moon. Must have heard it was made of green cheese. We never saw them again.

We stayed the afternoon—everyone did. Folks melted up buckets of prize butter, and someone went to town for barrels of salt. There was more than enough fresh popcorn to go around. Salted and buttered, it was delicious. One piece was enough to feed an entire family.

Did I tell you I'd as soon live in a tree as tamper with the truth? Well, when we got back that night, we found our farmhouse chawed and gnawed and eaten to the ground. Mr. Slim-Face John was not only tall, skinny, tangle-haired, and nearsighted. He was also color blind. Painted our house green.

Yes—it's a mite crowded living up here in the young'uns' tree house. But those prize ribbons–they're all mighty nice to look at.

SID FLEISCHMAN was awarded the 1987 Newbery Medal for *The Whipping Boy*. He was born in Brooklyn and grew up in San Diego. He worked as a professional magician and newspaperman before turning to fiction writing. He is a master of the comic novel, and his books have been translated into sixteen languages. A number of them have also been made into motion pictures.

His popular books include *The Whipping Boy, Jim Ugly, The Midnight Horse, The Ghost in the Noonday Sun, Mr. Mysterious & Company, Chancy and the Grand Rascal, Humbug Mountain, The Scarebird,* and *The Hey Hey Man.*

The father of three children (one of whom is the writer Paul Fleischman), he lives in Santa Monica, California.

QUENTIN BLAKE was born in London and attended Downing College, Cambridge. His cartoons and illustrations have appeared in *Punch, The Spectator,* and many other magazines. He began illustrating children's books in 1960. He is the author-artist of *Quentin Blake's ABC* and *All Join In,* among many other distingiushed books, and the illustrator of many of the stories of Roald Dahl as well as books by Joan Aiken and Russell Hoban. He lives in England.